# Collins

# Webster's

BESTSELLING BILINGUAL DICTIONARIES

# easy learning

# SPANISH

# IDIOMS

**HarperCollins Publishers**
Westerhill Road
Bishopbriggs
Glasgow
G64 2QT
Great Britain

First Edition 2011

Reprint 10 9 8 7 6 5 4 3 2 1

© HarperCollins Publishers 2011

Collins® is a registered trademark of
HarperCollins Publishers Limited

www.collinslanguage.com

A catalogue record for this book is
available from the British Library

ISBN 978-0-00-743773-3

Designed and typeset by
Thomas Callan

Printed in the USA by RR Donnelley

**Acknowledgements**
We would like to thank those authors
and publishers who kindly gave
permission for copyright material
to be used in the Collins Word Web.
We would also like to thank Times
Newspapers Ltd for providing valuable
data.

**PUBLISHING DIRECTOR**
Rob Scriven

**MANAGING EDITOR**
Gaëlle Amiot-Cadey

**PROJECT MANAGEMENT**
Susie Beattie
Jeremy Butterfield
Ben Harris

**CONTRIBUTORS**
José Antonio Gálvez Castiella
Sinda López Fuentes
Teresa Álvarez García
Talia Bugel

**ILLUSTRATION AND IMAGE RESEARCH**
Q2AMedia

# Introduction

## What is it?

*Collins Webster's Easy Learning Spanish Idioms* is an invaluable resource for learners of Spanish who want to be able to communicate more naturally. It will enable you to start to include colorful idiomatic phrases and expressions in both your writing and conversation, increasing your confidence and effectiveness. It can be used to develop your language skills, whether you are studying Spanish at school or college, at home or at an evening class.

## Why do you need it?

Developing expertise in writing, speaking, and understanding a foreign language means being able to pull together and build on a number of different aspects – vocabulary, grammar, pronunciation, and so on. An important element of increased proficiency in communication is the use of idioms and figurative expressions which will add color and variety to your writing and conversation as well as enable you to sound more natural and confident. Idioms are phrases whose meaning may not be obvious from the words they contain. For example, a common English idiom is "Add fuel to the fire." If somebody adds fuel to the fire, they make a bad situation worse.

## How is it structured?

*Easy Learning Spanish Idioms* has been carefully designed to provide a rich and easy-to-use resource for extending your language skills. It contains

250 phrases and expressions, all of which have been selected because they are commonly used by Spanish speakers today. These idioms are then grouped under 25 themes. Each of these themes covers an area of everyday life or experience, such as "Health, happiness, pleasure, and enjoyment," "Madness, foolishness, and stupidity," and "Directness, decisiveness, and expressing opinions."

Any idioms that are used only in Spain are indicated with (Sp). Latin American equivalents have been provided where necessary. Each idiom is followed by a word-for-word English translation as well as the equivalent idiomatic expression(s) that you would use in English. In many cases, a short background note is included if some explanation or additional information about Spanish language or culture is required. Then, in order to illustrate the use of the idiom in a natural context, a sentence or two of Spanish is provided. Again, this is translated into idiomatic English. For example:

## estar como unas castañuelas

*"to be like a pair of castanets"*
= to be as happy as a clam

What could be more typically Spanish than to use the cheerful, energizing sound of castanets to describe happiness?

**Está como unas castañuelas porque ha aprobado el examen.**
He's as happy as a clam because he's passed the exam.

## *Why choose* Collins Webster's Easy Learning Spanish Idioms?

- **easy to use**: 250 colorful idiomatic expressions arranged in 25 themes to do with daily life and common experience
- **easy to read**: a clear, modern layout which allows you to find the information you want quickly and easily
- **easy to understand**: written in an accessible style with the language you will hear from Spanish speakers today

# Contents

## Hope, dreams, fear, and anxiety

## Anger, annoyance, threats, and violence

## Truth, honesty, lying, and deceit

## Love, affection, marriage, and friendship

# Contents

## Argument, conflict, help, and cooperation

## Reprimands, praise, critics, and criticism

## Mistakes, shame, and embarrassment

## Knowledge, intelligence, ignorance, and understanding

## Looks, appearance, beauty, and vanity

## Insanity, foolishness, and stupidity

## Relationships, similarities, and differences

## Problems, difficulties, the possible, and the impossible

# Orders, obedience, control, and equality

# Work, achievement, effort, and ambition

## Change, continuity, risk, and opportunity

## Motion, travel, leaving, and parting

## Chance, surprise, and the unexpected

# Eating, drinking, drunkenness, and excess

# Directness, decisiveness, and expressing opinions

## Money, debt, wealth, and poverty

## Language, speech, silence, and conversation

## Youth, experience, age, and death

# Easy Learning Spanish Idioms

# Health, happiness, pleasure, and enjoyment

## estar como unas castañuelas

*"to be like a pair of castanets"*

= to be as happy as a clam

What could be more typically Spanish than to use the cheerful, energizing sound of castanets to describe happiness?

**Está como unas castañuelas porque ha aprobado el examen.**

He's as happy as a clam because he's passed the exam.

## estar más sano que una pera

*"to be healthier than a pear"*
= to be as fit as a fiddle

● Pears come into a couple of other colorful phrases in this book.

**Tiene ochenta años pero está más sano que una pera.**
He's eighty, but he's as fit as a fiddle.

## disfrutar como un enano (Sp)

*"to enjoy yourself like a dwarf"*
= to have a wonderful time

● Dwarves at the Spanish court kept the royal children company and led a privileged life, as can be seen in Spanish paintings of the seventeenth century, for instance by Velázquez. An equivalent of this expression, used more widely in the Spanish-speaking world, is **disfrutar como loco** (*to enjoy yourself like a crazy person*).

**José disfrutó como un enano en la playa.**
José had a wonderful time at the beach.

## tener cara de pascua (*Sp*)

*"to have an Easter face"*
= to be grinning from ear to ear

This phrase comes from the fact that Easter is a time of religious rejoicing.

**¡Qué suerte tuvo! No me sorprendió que tuviera cara de pascua.**
He was really lucky. I'm not surprised he was grinning from ear to ear.

# sobre gustos no hay nada escrito

> *"about taste there's nothing written down"*
> = there's no accounting for taste

You use this to suggest that something somebody else enjoys isn't really your cup of tea. It must be very old, as it is similar to a classic Latin phrase.

**Si a ti te encantó, me parece perfecto, sobre gustos no hay nada escrito.**
If you loved it, that's fine. There's no accounting for taste.

# hasta las tantas (Sp)

> *"until the so many (hours)"*
> = till all hours

Another version, used more widely in the Spanish-speaking world, is **hasta las mil** (*until the thousand (hours)*).

**Estuvimos charlando hasta las tantas.**
We were chatting till all hours.

## ser más fuerte que un roble

> *"to be stronger than an oak tree"*
> = to be as strong as an ox

If you're healthy and strong, you can also be described as
**más fuerte que un toro** (*stronger than a bull*).

**Es más fuerte que un roble. Consiguió mover el armario sin
pestañear.**
He's as strong as an ox. He managed to move the wardrobe
without batting an eye.

# Unhappiness, sickness, grief, and disappointment

## aburrirse como una ostra

*"to be as bored as an oyster"*
= to be bored stiff
= to be bored to death

Though oysters are a delicacy in the Spanish-speaking world, they don't have a very exciting life.

**Me aburro como una ostra, vámonos.**
I'm bored stiff; let's go.

## llevar a alguien por la calle de la amargura (Sp)

> *"to lead somebody down misery street"*
> = to make somebody's life miserable

**Desde que perdió el trabajo, su marido la lleva por la calle de la amargura.**
Ever since he lost his job, her husband has been making her life miserable.

## estar hasta las narices de algo/alguien

> *"to be up to the nostrils with something/somebody"*
> = to be fed up with something/somebody

Narices (*nostrils*) is the plural of nariz (*nose*). Another way of saying you're fed up is **estar hasta la coronilla** (*to be up to the crown of your head*).

**Estoy hasta las narices de sus impertinencias.**
I'm fed up with his insolence.

## tragar sapos

"*to swallow toads*"

= to go through hell

If you have to put up with something you don't like, swallowing toads conveys the idea nicely. Even more grisly is **tragar sapos y culebras** (*to swallow toads and snakes*).

**Tuvo que tragar sapos para conseguir salvar su matrimonio.**
He had to go through hell to save his marriage.

## no estar para fiestas

> *"not to be in the mood for parties"*
>
> = to be in no mood for fun and games

**Mejor salimos otro día, hoy no estoy para fiestas.**
It's best if we go out another day; I'm in no mood for fun and games.

## no tiene ni padre ni madre ni perrito que le ladre (Sp)

> *"he/she doesn't have a father or a mother or a little dog to bark for him/her"*
>
> = he/she is all alone in the world

● Like many colorful Spanish phrases, this one has a rhyme in it.

**Se ha quedado viudo y no tiene ni padre ni madre ni perrito que le ladre.**
He's been widowed, and he's all alone in the world.

## llorar como una magdalena

*"to cry like a Mary Magdalene"*

= to cry your eyes out

= to cry your heart out

This phrase comes from the grief of Mary Magdalene at the Crucifixion.

**Todos en el velatorio lloraban como una magdalena.**

Everyone at the wake was crying their eyes out.

## no estar muy católico

> *"not to be feeling very Catholic"*
> = to be feeling a little under the weather

**Hoy no estoy muy católico, me voy a acostar un rato.**
I'm feeling a little under the weather today. I think I'll lie down for a while.

## se le cayó el alma a los pies

> *"his soul sank to his feet"*
> = his heart sank

Many Spanish phrases refer to el alma where English talks about your *heart*. In this one, it could hardly sink any further.

**Cuando se enteró de la noticia, se le cayó el alma a los pies.**
When he heard the news, his heart sank.

# más se perdió en Cuba (Sp)

*"more was lost in Cuba"*
= it's not the end of the world
= worse things have happened

Cuba was the last Spanish colony, and its loss in 1898 was felt to be a catastrophe. If somebody has suffered a setback, you use this phrase to put it in perspective.

**¡Tranquilízate! No es una buena noticia, pero más se perdió en Cuba.**
Calm down! It may not be good news, but it's not the end of the world.

# Achievement, success, failure, and misfortune

## las vacas gordas

"*the fat cows*"
= boom years

● Though this seems like a farming image, it may actually come from the Bible, from Genesis.

**Se enriqueció durante las vacas gordas.**
He got rich during the boom years.

## poner una pica en Flandes (Sp)

*"to put a pike in Flanders"*
= to pull something off

● Spain fought campaigns in Flanders in the seventeenth century, but it was hard to get men to volunteer to fight there – to carry pikes.

**Ahora que leyó nuestra propuesta, ya hemos puesto una pica en Flandes.**
Now that he's read our proposal, I think we've basically pulled it off.

## ir viento en popa

*"to go wind in the stern"*
= to be going very well

● The image here comes from sailing. If the wind is coming from the stern of the boat, it fills the sails and the boat moves easily.

**El proyecto va viento en popa.**
The project is going very well.

## quedar en humo de paja

*"to end up as smoke from straw"*
= to come to nothing

**Esperemos que el acuerdo no quede en humo de paja.**
Let's hope that the agreement doesn't come to nothing.

## sacar agua de las piedras

*"to get water out of stones"*
= to work miracles

**Es una persona increíble, consigue sacar agua de las piedras.**
He's incredible. He manages to work miracles.

## no caerá esa breva (Sp)

> *"that early fig won't drop"*
> = in your dreams

The idea is that the fig isn't ripe enough to fall from the tree.

–A lo mejor se acuerda de ti y te invita.
–**No caerá esa breva.**
"Perhaps he'll remember you and invite you."
"In your dreams!"

## tener mala pata

> *"to have a bad leg"*
> = to be unlucky

Pata usually refers to an animal's leg but is also an informal word for a person's leg.

¡Qué mala pata tengo! He vuelto a perder el tren.
I'm so unlucky! I've missed the train again.

# ir sobre ruedas

### "to go on wheels"
= to go smoothly

The idea here is that if something is on wheels it runs smoothly.

**No te preocupes, que todo va sobre ruedas.**
Don't worry, everything's going smoothly.

## otro gallo te cantaría

*"another rooster would crow for you"*
= it would have been a different story

The reference here is religious: to the rooster that crowed when Saint Peter denied that he knew Jesus.

**Si hubiera estudiado más, otro gallo me cantaría.**
If I'd studied harder, it would have been a different story.

## llueve sobre mojado

*"it rains on what's already wet"*
= when it rains, it pours

**Primero la crisis mundial y ahora la gripe A: llueve sobre mojado.**
First the credit crunch, and now swine flu: when it rains, it pours.

# tirarse de las barbas (Sp)

### *"to tear your beard out"*
### = to be tearing your hair out

Beards appear in many phrases in Spanish culture, but you can also hear the exact equivalent of the English throughout the Spanish-speaking world: **tirarse de los pelos.**

**Se tiraba de las barbas por no haberse dado cuenta del error.**
He was tearing his hair out because he hadn't noticed the mistake.

## para más inri (*Sp*)

"*for more inri*"
= to top it all off
= to make matters worse

This is another religious reference. The Latin sign INRI
– standing for Jesus of Nazareth, King of the Jews – was
placed on the cross.

**Y, para más inri, ni siquiera se despidió.**
And, to top it all off, he didn't even say goodbye.

## éramos pocos y parió la abuela

"*there were only a few of us and grandma had a baby*"
= just when we thought things couldn't get any
worse
= that's all we needed
= that's just what we needed

If you picture a family struggling to make ends meet, and
then the grandmother has a baby too, it's hard to imagine
things getting any worse!

**Y ahora llega mi primo. ¡Éramos pocos y parió la abuela!**
And now here comes my cousin. That's all we needed!

# Hope, dreams, fear, and anxiety

## hacer las cuentas de la lechera

*"to do the milkmaid's sums"*
= to count your chickens before they're hatched

In a classic Spanish story, a milkmaid on her way to market daydreams about what she's going to do with her earnings. When she drops her milk, her dream is shattered.

**Tienes que ser más realista. Estás haciendo las cuentas de la lechera.**

You need to be more realistic. You're counting your chickens before they're hatched.

## esperar algo como agua de mayo (Sp)

> *"to hope for something like rain in May"*
> = to eagerly await something

In a dry country like Spain, rain in May is something that farmers long for to help their crops.

**Esperan** el anuncio de las ayudas públicas **como agua de mayo.**
They're eagerly awaiting the government's announcement of help.

## mi sueño dorado

> *"my golden dream"*
> = my dream

Something you really want in Spanish isn't merely a dream; it's a golden dream.

**El mundial es el sueño dorado de muchos futbolistas.**
The World Cup is many soccer players' dream.

## tener el alma en un hilo

"*to have your soul on a string*"
= to be worried sick

**Los padres del niño extraviado tienen el alma en un hilo.**
The missing child's parents are worried sick.


## no es tan fiero el león como lo pintan (Sp)

"*the lion is not as fierce as he is painted*"
= his bark is worse than his bite

A phrase with a similar meaning is **perro que ladra, poco muerde** (*a dog that barks doesn't bite much*), or even **perro que ladra, no muerde** (*a dog that barks doesn't bite*).

**Puedes hablar con él, no es tan fiero el león como lo pintan.**
You can speak to him: his bark is worse than his bite.

## liarse la manta a la cabeza (Sp)

> *"to tie your cape over your head"*
> = to take the plunge

You may be afraid, but if you tie your cape around your head you can't see the dangers that lie in wait.

**Un buen día, se lió la manta a la cabeza y se fue a vivir a Marruecos.**
One fine day, he took the plunge and went away to live in Morocco.

## hacer de tripas corazón

> *"to make a heart out of your guts"*
> = to pluck up the courage

**Hice de tripas corazón y le pedí perdón.**
I plucked up the courage and apologized to her.

## temblar como un flan

> *"to shake like a flan"*
> = to shake like a leaf

● Flan is a staple dessert in the Hispanic world, and can jiggle just as much as Jell-O.

**Cuando comenzó la entrevista, temblaba como un flan.**
At the beginning of the interview, I was shaking like a leaf.

# Anger, annoyance, threats, and violence

# estar hecho un ají

> *"to be a chili"*
> = to be fuming
> = to be hopping mad

● This expression is more commonly used in Latin America.

**Cuando me llamó, estaba hecho un ají.**
When he called me, he was fuming.

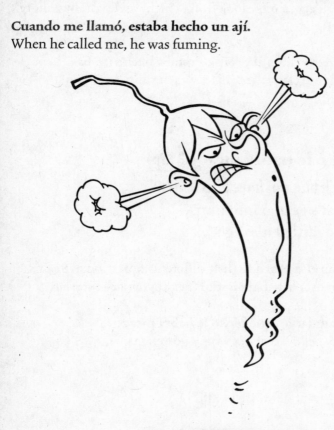

## estar hecho un basilisco

> "to be a basilisk"
> = to be fuming
> = to be hopping mad

● A basilisk is a mythical creature, hatched by a snake from a rooster's egg, a mere look from which was fatal. How angry is that?

**Cuando entré en clase, el profesor estaba hecho un basilisco.**
When I went into class, the teacher was fuming.

## ¿qué bicho le habrá picado? (Sp)

> "which bug can have bitten him?"
> = what's gotten into him?
> = who rattled his cage?

● You can also hear a slightly different expression in Spain: ¿qué mosca le habrá picado? (which fly can have bitten him?).

**No me ha saludado, ¿qué bicho le habrá picado?**
He didn't say hello. I wonder what's gotten into him?

# perder los estribos

*"to lose your stirrups"*
= to lose your temper
= to fly off the handle

The idea here is that your temper is like a horse you lose control of.

**Es una persona muy tranquila que nunca pierde los estribos.**
He's a very calm person who never flies off the handle.

# mandar a alguien a freír espárragos

*"to tell somebody to go and fry asparagus"*
= to tell somebody to get lost

There is another variation on this expression in Latin America: **mandar a alguien a bañarse** (*to tell somebody to go take a bath*).

**Me molestó tanto que acabé mandándola a freír espárragos.**
She annoyed me so much that in the end I told her to get lost.

# hacerse mala sangre

*"to make yourself bad blood"*
= to upset yourself
= to get hot under the collar

You mostly use this phrase in the negative, when telling somebody to calm down.

**No te hagas mala sangre, no vale la pena.**
Don't upset yourself; it's not worth it.

## soltar ajos y cebollas

*"to come out with garlics and onions"*

= to swear

= to let rip

● This expression is more commonly used in Latin America.

**Cuando veo cosas así, me entran ganas de soltar ajos y cebollas.**
Seeing things like that makes me want to let rip.

## tener cara de acelga (Sp)

> *"to have a face like Swiss chard"*
> = to get steamed up

How can a person who is annoyed look like a leaf vegetable? Swiss chard has a long, slender leaf, hence the image of a furious, long face. A colorful expression with the same meaning is used in the River Plate region of Latin America: **tener trompa** (*to have an elephant's trunk*).

**¿Por qué tienes esa cara de acelga?**
Why are you all steamed up?

# Truth, honesty, lying, and deceit

## dar a alguien gato por liebre

*"to give somebody cat instead of hare"*
= to sell somebody a bill of goods
= to pull a fast one on somebody

• Dishonest butchers used to sell cat meat as highly prized hare meat, especially after the Spanish Civil War, when food was scarce.

**Tengo bastante experiencia, no me vas a dar gato por liebre.**
I have quite a lot of experience – you're not going to pull a fast one on me.

## las mentiras tienen patas cortas

*"lies have short legs"*
= the truth will come to light

If you visualize lies as terriers with stumpy little legs, you'll quickly understand that they won't get very far.

**Hoy puede que consiga engañar a alguien, pero las mentiras tienen patas cortas.**
He might be able to get away with it today, but the truth will come to light.

## cuéntaselo a tu abuela

*"tell that to your grandmother"*
= tell me another

If you don't believe what somebody is saying, you can suggest they tell the same story to their grandmother, who will, of course, believe them! You need to know somebody very well to use this phrase.

**¿El autobús no pasó? ¡Cuéntaselo a tu abuela!**
The bus didn't come? Tell me another!

## tomar algo con pinzas

*"to take something with tongs"*
= to take something with a grain of salt

Just as you'd pick up something hot like a lump of coal with tongs, so you need to be very careful with what some people tell you.

**Yo esa afirmación la tomaría con pinzas.**
I would take that statement with a grain of salt.

## dale el pie y te tomará la mano (Sp)

> *"give him your foot and he'll take your hand"*
> = give him an inch and he'll take a mile

● This expression is slightly different in Latin America: **le das un dedo y te toma la mano** (*give him your finger and he'll take your hand*).

**Ten mucho cuidado con él, dale el pie y te tomará la mano.**
Be very careful with him: give him an inch and he'll take a mile.

## andar con mucho ojo

> *"to go with a lot of eye"*
> = to keep your wits about you
> = to be very careful

● Apart from its basic meaning of *eye*, **ojo** is used to mean *be careful*.

**Anda con mucho ojo que el centro de la ciudad es bastante peligroso.**
Keep your wits about you because the center of town is rather dangerous.

## untar la mano de alguien (Sp)

*"to grease somebody's hand"*
= to grease somebody's palm

**Se libró de la multa untando la mano del policía.**
He got out of paying by greasing the policeman's palm.

## no es trigo limpio

*"he isn't clean wheat"*
= he isn't to be trusted

**En esa oficina nadie es trigo limpio.**
No one can be trusted in that office.

## decir digo donde dije Diego (Sp)

*"to say 'digo' where I said 'Diego'"*
= to go back on your word

A tongue-twister and a pun at the same time.

**Nos prometió el viaje y ahora, donde dije digo, digo Diego.**
He promised us the trip, and now he's going back on his word.

# Love, affection, marriage, and friendship

# mi media naranja

*"my half orange"*
= my better half

- You can apply this expression to your better half, or to the person of your dreams that you're searching for.

**¿Puedo llevar a la fiesta a mi media naranja?**
Can I bring my better half to the party?

# beber los aires por alguien

> *"to drink the breezes for somebody"*
> = to be madly in love with somebody

● You can also use the expression **beber los vientos por alguien** (*to drink the winds for somebody*).

**Bebe los aires por una chica de su clase.**
He's madly in love with a girl in his class.


# pelar la pava (Sp)

> *"to peel the turkey"*
> = to whisper sweet nothings
> = to smooch

● The story goes that a maid was skinning a turkey by a window and spent ages chatting to her boyfriend there. When her mistress called, she replied: **Es que aún estoy pelando la pava** (*I'm still skinning the turkey*).

**Se pasaron la tarde pelando la pava.**
They spent the evening smooching.

## ser el ojo derecho de alguien (Sp)

*"to be somebody's right eye"*
= to be the apple of somebody's eye

Why the right eye? Because the right-hand side is
traditionally good and positive, as opposed to the left,
which is bad or sinister.

**Sara es el ojo derecho de la profesora.**
Sara is the apple of the teacher's eye.

## poner los cuernos a alguien

*"to put horns on somebody"*
= to cheat on somebody

Though no longer a prevalent image in English, horns are the traditional symbol of the cheated husband, often mentioned, for instance, in Shakespeare.

**Le pone los cuernos a su mujer.**
He's cheating on his wife.

## ser un pedazo de pan

*"to be a piece of bread"*
= to be a real sweetheart

Also common, and slightly more informal, is **ser un cacho de pan**.

**Mi hermana es un pedazo de pan.**
My sister is a real sweetheart.

## son como chanchos

*"they're like pigs"*
= they're as thick as thieves

**Se conocieron hace poco y ya son como chanchos.**
They only met recently, and already they're as thick as thieves.

## estar a partir un piñón (Sp)

> *"to be close enough to split a pine nut"*
> = to be bosom buddies

Pine nuts, occasionally used in Hispanic cooking, are even smaller than peanuts. You'd have to be really good friends to share one.

**Mi hermana y Julia están a partir un piñón.**
My sister and Julia are bosom buddies.

## hacer buenas migas

> *"to make good crumbs"*
> = to hit it off

The story behind this very old phrase is this: shepherds made a simple meal of fat and **migas** (*crumbs*). If the ingredients are good they bind well together, just like good friends.

**Los niños hicieron buenas migas rápidamente.**
The children hit it off very quickly.

# Argument, conflict, help,
# and cooperation

## no apearse del burro

*"not to get down from your donkey"*
= to refuse to back down

● A variation, more commonly used in Latin America, is **no apearse del caballo**. (*not to get down, from your horse*).

**Hemos intentado dialogar con ella pero no se apea del burro.**
We've tried to talk to her, but she refuses to back down.

## se armó la de San Quintín

*"what happened at San Quintín broke out"*
= there was an almighty ruckus
= all hell broke loose

This venerable phrase refers to the Spanish taking the French town of Saint Quentin in a bloody battle, in 1557. It was to commemorate this great victory that Philip II ordered the famous palace **El Escorial** to be built.

**Cuando el profesor salió de la clase, se armó la de San Quintín.**
When the teacher left the classroom, all hell broke loose.

## llevar el agua a su molino

*"to lead the water to your own mill"*
= to turn things to your own advantage

Water being historically a scarce resource, there were often disputes over who used it, and crafty millers would divert it.

**Es normal que cada uno quiera llevar el agua a su molino.**
It's normal for everyone to want to turn things to their own advantage.

# arrimar el ascua a su sardina

*"to put the coals close to your own sardine"*
= to look out for number one

Obviously, if several people are barbecuing sardines and you put yours nearest the coals, it will cook first. Very selfish.

**Es de los que siempre intenta arrimar el ascua a su sardina.**
He's one of those people who always try to look out for number one.

# echar pelillos a la mar (Sp)

*"to throw little hairs into the sea"*
= to bury the hatchet

"But I thought **el mar** was masculine," I hear you say. You are absolutely right. But in some phrases it becomes the feminine **la mar**, as here.

**Pues nos damos un abrazo y echamos pelillos a la mar.**
Well, let's give each other a hug and bury the hatchet.

# nunca llueve a gusto de todos

*"it never rains to everyone's taste"*

= you can never please everybody

**Como nunca llueve a gusto de todos, hubo unos pocos que protestaron por la decisión.**
As you can never please everybody, there were a few people who complained about the decision.

# decir amén a todo

*"to say amen to everything"*

= to say yes to everything

= to be a yes-man

**Aunque no estés de acuerdo, tú di amén a todo.**
Even if you don't agree, just say yes to everything.

## tener a alguien entre ceja y ceja

*"to have somebody between eyebrow and eyebrow"*
= to have it in for somebody

A related phrase with the same meaning is **tener a alguien entre ojos** *(to have somebody between your eyes)*.

**Tengo a Carlos entre ceja y ceja.**
I've got it in for Carlos.

## romper una lanza a favor de alguien

*"to break a lance for somebody"*

= to stick your neck out for somebody

**Quería romper una lanza a favor del** criticado presidente.
I wanted to stick my neck out for the president, who had been criticized.

# Reprimands, praise, critics, and criticism

## poner a alguien por las nubes

*"to put somebody in the clouds"*
= to praise somebody to the skies

● The English and Spanish phrases are very similar, but the Spanish is more specific.

**En la reseña ponen al director por las nubes.**
In the review, the director is praised to the skies.

# leer la cartilla a alguien (Sp)

> "to read the primer to somebody"
> = to read somebody the riot act
> = to take somebody to task

In olden days, **cartillas** (*primers*) were very simple books with the ABC's from which children learned to read and write. If you read it out to somebody, you're making sure they remember it.

**Si no apruebo todas, mis padres me van a leer la cartilla.**
If I don't pass all my classes, my parents are going to read me the riot act.

# poner a alguien como un trapo (Sp)

> "to leave somebody like a rag"
> = to tear somebody to shreds

**Cuando descubrió lo que había hecho, el profesor me puso como un trapo.**
When he found out what I'd done, the teacher really tore me to shreds.

## ser canela fina

*"to be fine cinnamon"*
= to be first-rate
= to be stellar

**El reparto de esa película es canela fina.**
The cast of that movie is stellar.


## que da gloria

*"that gives glory"*
= wonderfully

**Cocina que da gloria.**
She's a wonderful cook.

# lo dijo de boca para fuera

> *"he said it from the mouth outward"*
> = he didn't really mean it

● You use this very physical phrase to criticize somebody by suggesting that they are insincere. Another variation is **lo dijo de labios para fuera** (*he said it from the lips outward*).

**Afirmó que estaba encantado pero sé que lo dijo de boca para fuera.**
He said he was delighted, but I know he didn't really mean it.

# no tener nombre

> *"not to have a name"*
> = to be unspeakable
> = to be despicable

**Lo que hicieron contigo no tiene nombre.**
What they did to you is despicable.

## hablar pestes de alguien

*"to talk plagues about somebody"*
= to bad-mouth somebody
= to put somebody down

**Siempre que no está delante, habla pestes de su suegra.**
Whenever she's not around, he bad-mouths his mother-in-law.

## regalar el oído a alguien (Sp)

*"to regale somebody's ears"*
= to flatter somebody

**Elógiale, le encanta que le regalen el oído.**
Praise him; he loves to be flattered.

## de mala muerte

*"of a bad death"*

= awful

= horrible

**Tuvimos que pasar la noche en un hotel de mala muerte.**
We had to spend the night in an awful hotel.

# Mistakes, shame, and embarrassment

## ser como guitarra en un entierro

*"to be like a guitar at a funeral"*
= to be completely out of place
= to stick out like a sore thumb

**Con esa ropa eres como una guitarra en un entierro.**
With those clothes on, you're completely out of place.

## meter la pata

> *"to put your leg"*
> = to put your foot in it

Pata is an informal word for leg. You can also use another slang word for leg in the expression **meter la gamba**.

**Creo que he metido la pata.**
I think I've put my foot in it.

## como un tomate

> *"as red as a tomato"*
> = as red as a beet

You can also say **rojo como un tomate**.

**Al subir al escenario se puso como un tomate.**
When he got up on stage, he turned beet red.

## ponerse como un ají

*"to look like a chili"*

= to turn bright red

**Cuando la chica le sonrió, se puso como un ají.**
When the girl smiled at him, he turned bright red.

## fulminar a alguien con la mirada

*"to strike somebody with lightning with a look"*
= to shoot somebody a dirty look

● This is the kind of withering look you give somebody who has just done or said something very indiscreet.

**Le interrumpí sin querer y me fulminó con la mirada.**
I interrupted him without meaning to, and he shot me a dirty look.

# quedar a la altura del betún (Sp)

*"to be left at the height of shoe polish"*
= to make yourself look really bad

If you've done something embarrassing, it would be hard to feel much lower than the polish on your shoes.

**Con sus insultos quedó a la altura del betún.**
His insults made him look really bad.

# Knowledge, intelligence, ignorance, and understanding

# haberse caído del guindo (Sp)

*"to have fallen out of the cherry tree"*
= to have been born yesterday

● A fig tree is used instead in different parts of the Spanish-speaking world: **haberse caído de la higuera**.

**¿No te pensarás que me he caído del guindo?**
Do you think I was born yesterday?

## ser más listo que Lepe (Sp)

"*to be smarter than Lepe*"

= to be pretty smart

The Lepe in question was a seventeenth-century Spanish bishop famed for his vast learning and intelligence – the Einstein of his day. Remember that with **ser**, **listo** means *smart*, but with **estar** it means *ready*.

**Ese primo tuyo es más listo que Lepe.**
That cousin of yours is pretty smart.

## saber la biblia en verso

"*to know the Bible in verse*"

= to know absolutely everything

A very untalented nineteenth-century Spanish writer versified part of the Bible, which gave rise to this phrase, often with a suggestion of something long and tedious.

**Pregúntale cualquier cosa, se sabe la biblia en verso.**
Ask him anything; he knows absolutely everything.

## ser una lanza (Sp)

*"to be a lance"*

= to be really on the ball

A similar expression is used in Latin America: **ser un rayo** (*to be a lightning bolt*).

**Puede que parezca tonto, pero ese chico es una lanza.**
He may seem stupid, but that boy is really on the ball.

## conocer algo como la palma de la mano

*"to know something like the palm of your hand"*

= to know something like the back of your hand

This is another phrase where Spanish and English are similar yet subtly different.

**Se conoce la ciudad como la palma de la mano.**
He knows the city like the back of his hand.

## no saber ni jota de algo (Sp)

*"not to know even letter j about something"*

= not to know the first thing about something

Another phrase to convey the same idea is **no saber ni papa de algo** (*not to know even a potato about something*) or, in Latin America, **no saber un pepino de algo** (*not to know a cucumber about something*).

**No sabe ni jota de informática.**
He doesn't know the first thing about computer science.

## oír campanas y no saber de dónde vienen

*"to hear bells and not know where they're coming from"*

= not to have a clue

In this phrase, notice how the question word **dónde** has an accent.

**Ese ha oído campanas y no sabe de dónde vienen.**
He doesn't have a clue.

## ser un águila

> *"to be an eagle"*
> = to be very sharp

●  This refers to being sharp in general, not merely to being eagle-eyed.

**Es un águila y ve las oportunidades donde los demás no vemos nada.**
He's very sharp, and he sees opportunities where the rest of us don't see anything.

## no saber de qué va la fiesta (Sp)

> *"not to know what the party's about"*
> = to be clueless

In this phrase, notice how the question word qué has an accent.

**Si quieres que te diga la verdad, no sé de qué va la fiesta.**
To tell you the truth, I'm clueless.

## no saber de la misa la media

> *"not to know half the mass"*
> = not to have a clue

You can also say **no saber de la misa la mitad.**

**Habla mucho pero no sabe de la misa la media.**
He talks a lot, but he doesn't have a clue.

# tomar el rábano por las hojas

*"to take hold of the radish by the leaves"*
= to get it all wrong

If you start eating the leaves of a radish, you obviously don't know how to eat radishes – or, it is implied, much else.

**Estás tomando el rábano por las hojas. ¿Por qué no me escuchas?**
You are getting it all wrong.
Why don't you listen to me?

# lo saben hasta las piedras

"*even stones know that*"
= it's common knowledge
= everyone knows that

**Están saliendo juntos, lo saben hasta las piedras.**
They're going out together; everyone knows that.

# me suena a chino

"*it sounds like Chinese to me*"
= it's all Greek to me

**Esas instrucciones me suenan a chino.**
Those instructions are all Greek to me.

# Looks, appearance, beauty, and vanity

## estar hecho un espárrago

"*to be an asparagus*"
= to be as skinny as a rail
= to be thin as a rail

● Here is another Spanish idiom using a food analogy. Another phrase used to describe somebody thin is **estar como un fideo** (*to be like a spaghetti*), and in Latin America you might also hear **estar como un alfiler** (*to be like a pin*).

**Debería comer más, está hecho un espárrago.**
He should eat more; he's thin as a rail.

## el hábito no hace al monje

> *"the habit doesn't make the monk"*
> = don't judge somebody by his/her appearance
> = don't judge a book by its cover

**Puede que no parezca un profesional, pero el hábito no hace al monje.**
He may not look like a professional, but you shouldn't judge a man by his appearance.

## estar hecho un Adán (Sp)

> *"to be like Adam"*
> = to look a mess
> = to look like something the cat dragged in

**Estás hecho un Adán, ¿no pensarás ir a la fiesta así?**
You look a mess. You're not thinking of going to the party like that, are you?

## tener ángel

*"to have angel"*
= to have charm
= to be very charming

● You can apply this expression to
somebody who has great charm, even
if they are not good-looking.
The idea is an angel must
be looking after them.

**Esa chica tiene ángel.**
That girl is very charming.

# más feo que Picio (Sp)

"*uglier than Picio*"
= as ugly as sin

Picio, poor guy, appears to have been a real person in nineteenth-century Spain. Another expression is **feo como un grajo** (*as ugly as a rook*).

**Su novio es más feo que Picio.**
Her boyfriend is as ugly as sin.

# no necesitar abuela (Sp)

"*not to need a grandmother*"
= to be full of yourself
= to blow your own horn

Grandparents dote on their grandchildren, and praise whatever they do. So if somebody doesn't need a grandmother to praise them, it's because they do it themselves!

**Ese no necesita abuela, siempre elogiándose.**
He is so full of himself he doesn't need anyone else to praise him.

## tener la cabeza como una bola de billar

*"to have your head like a billiard ball"*
= to be as bald as a cue ball

What could be more lacking in hair than a billiard ball?

**Lo reconocerás fácilmente porque tiene la cabeza como una bola de billar.**
You'll easily recognize him because he's as bald as a cue ball.

## un hombre de pelo en pecho

*"a man with hair on his chest"*

= a real man

**Dice que quiere un hombre de pelo en pecho.**
She says she wants a real man.

# chupar cámara (Sp)

*"to suck the camera"*
= to get a lot of media attention

This sarcastic phrase refers to politicians, celebrities, and others – you know who they are – who love being filmed and photographed at every possible opportunity.

**Es uno de esos políticos a los que les gusta chupar cámara.**
He's one of those politicians who like to get a lot of media attention.

# Insanity, foolishness, and stupidity

# estar más loco que una cabra

### "to be crazier than a goat"
= to be as crazy as a loon
= to be as mad as a hatter

● A goat's behavior is somewhat unpredictable, hence the image.

**Mi profesor de física está más loco que una cabra.**
My physics teacher is as crazy as a loon.

## estar mal de la azotea (Sp)

> *"to have a problem on your roof terrace"*
> = to be out of your mind
> = to have bats in your belfry

**Azoteas** are the tiled terraces that you might see on traditional houses with flat roofs. As coconuts are often used to refer to heads throughout the Spanish-speaking world, you might also hear **estar mal del coco** (*to have a problem in your coconut*).

**Tú estás mal de la azotea, ¿cómo se te ocurre decir esa tontería?**
You're out of your mind. How can you talk such nonsense?

## estar como una regadera (Sp)

> *"to be like a watering can"*
> = to have a screw loose

What's the connection? The idea is that the head on the spout of a watering can has lots of little holes in it, as does the head, figuratively speaking, of the person you're referring to.

**Mi tío está como una regadera.**
My uncle has a screw loose.

# estar loco de atar

*"to be crazy enough to tie up"*
= to be stark raving mad
= to be out of your mind

**¿Estás loco de atar?, ¿quieres que nos castiguen?**
Are you out of your mind? Do you want them to punish us?

# perder la chaveta

*"to lose your pin"*
= to lose your head
= to flip out

**Intenté tranquilizarle pero perdió la chaveta.**
I tried to calm him down, but he flipped out.

## estar en la luna de Valencia

> *"to be in the Valencia moon"*
> = to be daydreaming

Valencia is an important port city in Spain, and some believe that the origin of this expression dates from medieval times when the walls of the city were closed at night, leaving those outside with only the moon as shelter.

**Estás en la luna de Valencia, ¿o qué?**
Are you daydreaming or what?

## estar en Babia

> *"to be in Babia"*
> = to be on another planet

What and where is Babia? One suggestion is that it was where a medieval Spanish king went to to get away from the Court. Over time, the phrase came to mean mental rather than physical absence.

**Parece que estés en Babia, ¿te has enterado de lo que he dicho?**
You seem to be on another planet. Did you get what I said?

## tener pájaros en la cabeza (Sp)

*"to have birds in your head"*

= to be an airhead

**No le hagas mucho caso, tiene pájaros en la cabeza.**
Don't take any notice of him: he's an airhead.

## más bruto que un arado

*"more stupid than a plow"*
= as dumb as an ox

**No dejes que toque el ordenador, es más bruto que un arado.**
Don't let him touch the computer; he's as dumb as an ox.

## ser un animal de bellota (*Sp*)

*"to be an animal of acorns"*
= to be thick-headed

The most highly prized Spanish ham is **jamón de bellota** (*acorn ham*). It comes from pigs which are left to wander freely in oak forests to fatten up.

**Eres un animal de bellota, te lo voy a explicar otra vez.**
You're really thick-headed. Let me explain it to you again.

## ser de pocas luces

> *"to have few lights"*
> = to be not very bright

**No esperes mucho de ella, es de pocas luces.**
Don't expect a lot of her; she's not very bright.


## no tener dos dedos de frente

> *"not to have two fingers' width of forehead"*
> = not to have any brains

**Parece que no tiene dos dedos de frente.**
He doesn't seem to have any brains.

# Relationships, similarities, and differences

## son lobos de una camada

> *"they're wolves of one litter"*
> = they're birds of a feather

**No te quejes de tus compañeros que sois todos lobos de una camada.**
Don't complain about your classmates; you're all birds of a feather.

## ni de aquí a Lima (Sp)

*"not from here to Lima"*
= there's just no comparison
= not by a long shot

The vast distance between Spain and Lima, the capital of Peru, emphasizes the difference between the things you're talking about.

**Maradona no fue mejor que Pelé, ni de aquí a Lima.**
Maradona wasn't better than Pelé – not by a long shot.

## no es santo de mi devoción

*"he's not a saint of my devotion"*
= he's not my kind of person

People often have a saint that they're particularly devoted to.

**Sabes perfectamente que tu hermano no es santo de mi devoción.**
You know perfectly well that your brother's not my kind of person.

## ser uña y carne (Sp)

> *"to be nail and flesh"*
> = to be inseparable
> = to be joined at the hip

● This expression is sometimes reversed in Latin America: ser carne y uña.

**Elsa y Clara son uña y carne.**
Elsa and Clara are inseparable.

## cojean del mismo pie (Sp)

> *"they limp with the same foot"*
> = they're two of a kind

● In some Latin American countries, this expression becomes renguean del mismo pie, which has the same meaning.

**Los dos cojean del mismo pie y no saben decir que no a una botella de vino.**
They're two of a kind, and they can't say no to a bottle of wine.

# Dios los cría y ellos se juntan

*"God brings them up and they get together"*
= birds of a feather flock together

**Todos sus amigos son también programadores: Dios los cría y ellos se juntan.**
All his friends are programmers too – birds of a feather flock together.

# no hay que confundir la gimnasia con la magnesia (Sp)

*"you must not confuse gymnastics and magnesium"*
= let's not mix up two totally different things
= let's not confuse matters

**No hay que confundir la gimnasia con la magnesia, una cosa es ser franco, otra es ser grosero.**
Let's not confuse matters. It's one thing to be frank, and another to be rude.

## me cae gordísimo

*"he falls on me very very fat"*
= I can't stand him

The **ísimo** ending on an adjective means "very, very:"
**Es altísimo** (He's *very, very* tall).

**La nueva profesora de química me cae gordísima.**
I can't stand the new chemistry teacher.

## no se parecen ni en el blanco de los ojos

> *"they don't resemble each other even in the whites of their eyes"*
>
> = to be like night and day

**Mis hermanas no se parecen ni en el blanco de los ojos.**
My sisters are as different as night and day.

# Problems, difficulties, the possible, and the impossible

## cuando las ranas críen pelo (Sp)

*"when frogs will grow hair"*
= when pigs fly

In Latin America, you might hear the phrase **el día del arquero** (*on goalkeeper's day*). Although there is a mother's day and a father's day, there is no goalkeeper's day, so you can use this expression to refer to something that will never happen.

· **Te dejaré el dinero cuando las ranas críen pelo.**
Yeah, I'll lend you the money – when pigs fly!

## ahogarse en un vaso de agua

*"to drown in a glass of water"*

= to make a mountain out of a molehill

**Mi madre es de las que se ahoga en un vaso de agua.**
My mother's one of those people who make mountains out of molehills.

## ir de Guatemala a Guatepeor

*"to go from Guatebad to Guateworse"*

= to jump out of the frying pan and into the fire

This is a pun on the name of the Central American country. **Malo** means *bad*, and its comparative is **peor**, meaning *worse*.

**Con este nuevo gobierno vamos de Guatemala a Guatepeor.**
With this new government, we're jumping out of the frying pan and into the fire.

## estar entre la espada y la pared

> "to be between the sword and the wall"
> = to be between a rock and a hard place

**Estoy entre la espada y la pared, y sinceramente no sé qué hacer.**
I'm caught between a rock and a hard place, and honestly I don't
know what to do.

## no hay mal que por bien no venga

> "there is no bad that doesn't turn out well"
> = every cloud has a silver lining

Why the subjunctive **venga**? Because it follows **no hay**. You
use the subjunctive to say that something doesn't exist, or
isn't the case: **No tiene a nadie que le ayude** (*He doesn't have
anybody to help him*).

**No hay mal que por bien no venga: esa lluvia es una bendición
para el campo.**
Every cloud has a silver lining: that rain is a blessing for the
countryside.

# pedir peras al olmo

> *"to ask the elm tree for pears"*
> = to ask for the impossible

'Here's another phrase with pears. What could be more impossible than expecting an elm tree to produce them?

**Querer que Carlos saque buenas notas es pedir peras al olmo.**
Wanting Carlos to get good grades is asking for the impossible.

# a perro flaco todo son pulgas

> *"to a thin dog it's all fleas"*
> = when it rains, it pours

**A perro flaco todo son pulgas: primero las piedras en el riñón y ahora el cáncer.**
When it rains, it pours: first kidney stones, and now cancer.

## meter palos en las ruedas

*"to put sticks in the wheels"*

= to throw a monkey wrench in the works

= to trip somebody up

**El presidente pidió a la oposición que esta vez no metiera palos en las ruedas.**

The president asked the opposition
not to throw a monkey wrench
in the works this time.

## es pan comido (Sp)

*"it's bread that's been eaten"*
= it's a piece of cake

**No te preocupes que esto es pan comido, te lo arreglo en cinco minutos.**
Don't worry, this is a piece of cake. I can fix it for you in five minutes.

## no todo el monte es orégano (Sp)

*"not all the hillside is oregano"*
= life isn't a bed of roses

Oregano can grow wild on the hills, and makes good grazing for sheep and goats.

**Cuando crezcas descubrirás que no todo el monte es orégano.**
When you grow up, you'll find out that life isn't a bed of roses.

## esto no tiene mucha ciencia

> *"this doesn't have a lot of science"*
> = there's nothing to it

**Lo voy a resolver rápidamente porque esto no tiene mucha ciencia.**
It won't take me long to fix because there's nothing to it.

## no lo voy a hacer ni loco

> *"I'm not going to do it even if crazy"*
> = nothing in the world would make me do it

● You use this phrase when there really is no way you'll do something.

**No voy a pedirle perdón ni loco.**
Nothing in the world would make me apologize to him.

## parece mentira que ...

> *"it seems a lie that ..."*
> = I can't believe that ...
> = It seems impossible that ...

● Notice how you use the subjunctive after this phrase.

**Parece mentira que tenga que repetir esto todos los días.**
I can't believe I have to say the same thing every day.

## a buenas horas mangas verdes (Sp)

> *"in good time green sleeves"*
> = it's too late now

● You use this to criticize somebody who offers help but turns up too late to be of any use. In the fifteenth century, the rural police in Spain wore uniforms with green sleeves – and they were notorious for turning up too late, after the event.

**A buenas horas mangas verdes, tu invitación ya no me sirve.**
It's too late now; your invitation's no use to me anymore.

## en dos patadas

*"in two kicks"*
= in a flash
= in no time

**Llegaré ahí en dos patadas.**
I'll be there in no time.

# Orders, obedience, control, and equality

## pagar el pato

"*to pay for the duck*"

= to be stuck holding the bag

**¿Por qué tengo que ser yo el que siempre pague el pato?**
Why do I always have to be the one who's stuck holding the bag?

## tener la sartén por el mango

> *"to hold the frying pan by the handle"*
> = to call the shots
> = to be the boss

**Aquí en casa la que tiene la sartén por el mango es ella.**
She's the one who calls the shots at home.

## cortar el bacalao

> *"to cut the bacalao"*
> = to be in charge
> = to call the shots

**Bacalao** is dried, salted cod, still used in some typical
Hispanic dishes. Before refrigeration, fish was dried and
salted to preserve it, and the person entrusted with cutting
such a delicacy was clearly in charge.

**Quiero hablar con el que realmente corta el bacalao aquí.**
I want to speak to the person who's really in charge here.

# tener a alguien más derecho que una vela (Sp)

*"to have somebody straighter than a sail"*
= to have somebody under your thumb

Spain has many phrases that derive from its seafaring history. There is an equivalent expression used in many Spanish-speaking countries: **tener a alguien con las riendas cortas** (*to have somebody on short reins*).

**El profesor de inglés los tiene más derechos que una vela.**
The English teacher's really got them under his thumb.

# pagar los platos rotos

*"to pay for the broken plates"*
= to pay for it

A phrase to be used when somebody takes the rap for something that is not their fault.

**Esta vez va a ser mi hermana la que pague los platos rotos.**
This time it's going to be my sister who pays for it.

# cargar con el muerto

> *"to carry the dead man"*
> = to take the blame

In medieval Spain, if the body of someone who met a violent death was found, and the culprit was not discovered, the locals would have to pay a fine. To avoid this, they would carry the body and dump it within the boundaries of the next village or town.

**Pueden buscar a otro porque no pienso cargar con el muerto.**
They can look for somebody else because I have no intention of taking the blame.

# tener a alguien metido en el bote (Sp)

> *"to have somebody put in the jar"*
> = to have somebody eating out of your hand

Throughout the Spanish-speaking world, you will also hear **tener a alguien metido en el bolsillo,** and in Mexico you will hear **tener a alguien metido en el bolso.** Both mean *to have somebody put in the pocket.*

**Tengo a mi jefe metido en el bote.**
I've got my boss eating out of my hand.

# llevar la batuta

*"to carry the baton"*
= to be in charge

The baton here is a conductor's baton.

**Yo soy el que llevo la batuta en la oficina.**
I'm the one who's in charge in the office.

## al pie de la letra

*"to the foot of the letter"*

= to the letter

= exactly

**Seguí las instrucciones al pie de la letra.**
I followed the instructions to the letter.

## bailar el agua a alguien (Sp)

*"to dance the water to somebody"*

= to suck up to somebody

**Siempre les ha bailado el agua a los jefes.**
He's always sucked up to the bosses.

# bailar al son que tocan

*"to dance to the tune they're playing"*
= to toe the line

**Estamos acostumbrados a bailar al son que tocan.**
We're used to toeing the line.

# Work, achievement, effort, and ambition

## trabajar como un burro

*"to work like a donkey"*
= to work like a horse
= to work your fingers to the bone

Donkeys feature in many colorful phrases, such as this one.

**Trabajé como un burro para entregar la redacción a tiempo.**
I worked my fingers to the bone to hand in the essay on time.

## tirar del carro

"*to pull the cart*"
= to do the donkeywork
= to do the grunt work

**Siempre tiene que haber alguien que tire del carro.**
There always has to be somebody to do the donkeywork.

## trabajar como una hormiga

"*to work like an ant*"
= to work very hard
= to slave away

**Acumuló una pequeña fortuna después de trabajar como una hormiga durante décadas.**
She amassed a small fortune after working very hard for decades.

# ganarse los garbanzos (Sp)

*"to earn your chickpeas"*

= to earn a living

= to earn your keep

A similar expression used in Spain is **ganarse las lentejas** (*to earn your lentils*) or, in Latin America, **ganarse los frijoles** (*to earn your beans*).

**Acepta cualquier tipo de trabajo porque, como todo el mundo, tiene que ganarse los garbanzos.**

He accepts any kind of work because, like everybody, he needs to earn a living.

# un trabajo de chinos

*"a job for Chinese people"*
= painstaking work

Chinese decorative goods – such as porcelain and lacquerware – were highly prized historically in Europe. This phrase refers to the patience needed to make these delicate, detailed, and exquisite objects.

**Montar la estantería fue un auténtico trabajo de chinos.**
Putting up the bookcase was really painstaking work.

# unos cardan la lana y otros cobran la fama (Sp)

*"some card the wool and others gain the glory"*
= some do all the work and others take all the credit

Carding wool involves cleaning and combing it to make it suitable for weaving: extremely hard manual labor, before machines were invented to do the job.

**Todos sabemos de quién fue el mérito, pero unos cardan la lana y otros cobran la fama.**
We all know who the credit belongs to, but some do all the work, and others take all the credit.

## no se ganó Zamora en una hora (Sp)

*"Zamora was not won in an hour"*
= Rome wasn't built in a day

You use this rhyming phrase to remind people that achieving something worthwhile takes time. The town of Zamora lies in the autonomous region of Castille and León, in northwest Spain, and was the site of an epic siege in the eleventh century.

**Vamos con calma, que no se ganó Zamora en una hora.**
Let's take things slowly. Rome wasn't built in a day.

## quemarse las pestañas

*"to singe your eyelashes"*
= to burn the midnight oil

You can imagine studying by lamp- or candlelight, and being so near the flame that you singe your eyelashes. The reflexive **quemarse** is used, as with so many actions referring to parts of the body.

**Se ha quemado las pestañas durante un mes para preparar el examen.**
He burned the midnight oil for a month studying for the exam.

## se le va la fuerza por la boca

> *"his strength goes out through his mouth"*
> = he's all talk and no action

**Es muy bravucón pero se le va la fuerza por la boca.**
He's full of bluster, but he's all talk and no action.


## poner toda la carne en el asador

> *"to put all the meat on the barbecue"*
> = to pull out all the stops

If you put all your meat on the grill at the same time, you leave nothing for later.

**Vamos a tener que poner toda la carne en el asador si queremos derrotarlos.**
We're going to have to pull out all the stops if we want to beat them.

## rascarse la barriga

*"to scratch your belly"*
= to do nothing
= to sit on your backside

**No te quedes ahí sentado rascándote la barriga y ven a ayudarme.**
Don't just sit there on your backside: come and help me.

## sacar fuerzas de flaqueza

*"to pull strength out of weakness"*
= to use all your energy

**Tuve que sacar fuerzas de flaqueza para conseguir llegar a la cumbre.**
I had to use all my energy to manage to get to the summit.

# Change, continuity, risk, and opportunity

# ser un culo de mal asiento (Sp)

*"to be a backside that can't sit still"*
= to have ants in your pants

● The Latin American equivalent, tener hormigas en el trasero (*to have ants on your backside*), is much closer to the English.

¡Pero **qué culo de mal asiento eres!** ¿No te podrías quedar quieto un rato?
Do you have ants in your pants? Can't you sit still for a minute?

## entre col y col, lechuga (Sp)

*"betweeen cabbage and cabbage, lettuce"*
= variety is the spice of life
= for a change

Legend has it that a particular Spanish king used to eat cabbage salads in order to lose weight, and sometimes lettuce would be added for a bit of variety in his diet!

**Entre col y col, lechuga: vamos a hacer un inciso para hablar de arte.**
For a change, we're going to digress and talk about art.

## borrón y cuenta nueva

*"crossing out and a new sum"*
= let's start over
= let's make a fresh start

If you make a mistake while doing a math problem, you cross it out and start over. This phrase suggests the same applies to life.

**Le pides perdón y borrón y cuenta nueva.**
Apologize to her and make a fresh start.

# a otra cosa, mariposa

*"to something else, butterfly"*
= let's move on to something else

⬤ You use this phrase to emphasize that a particular topic or event is over. Its rhyme gives it a suitable finality.

**Vamos a acabar de leer este capítulo, y a otra cosa, mariposa.**
Let's finish reading this chapter, and then move on to something else.

# cambiar el chip

*"to change the chip"*
= to change your attitude toward something

⬤ With its reference to microchips, this phrase is clearly modern. The idea is that your mind is an electronic device, and by putting in a different chip you can change your outlook.

**Ya es hora de que cambies el chip y te des cuenta de que estás en la universidad.**
It's time to change your attitude and realize that you're in college.

# la ocasión la pintan calva (Sp)

"*they depict opportunity as bald*"
= you have to grab the opportunity

**Ocasión** can mean an opportunity as well as an occasion. The phrase relates to the image of opportunity as a goddess. She's bald because in Spanish you have to *seize opportunity by the hair* (**coger la ocasión por los pelos**).

**Me presenté candidato de inmediato porque la ocasión la pintan calva.**
I applied right away, because you have to grab the opportunity when it presents itself.

# hay moros en la costa

"*there are Moors on the coast*"
= watch out

Much of the Spanish coast is within easy distance of North Africa, and historically Moorish pirates from there raided Spanish ports. This phrase is a warning that an adult or somebody in authority is around.

**Esconde el cigarrillo que hay moros en la costa.**
Watch out! Somebody's coming. Hide the cigarette.

# no está el horno para bollos

> *"the oven isn't ready for buns"*
> = the time isn't right

**Yo no discutiría el asunto con nuestros padres, no está el horno para bollos.**
I wouldn't talk about it with Mom and Dad; the time isn't right.

# Motion, travel, leaving, and parting

# en el quinto infierno

*"in the fifth hell"*

= in the middle of nowhere

This diabolical image has a colorful Latin American version: **donde el diablo perdió el poncho** (*where the Devil lost his poncho*).

**Vive en el quinto infierno.**
He lives in the middle of nowhere.

## a toda mecha (Sp)

*"at full fuse"*
= like greased lightning

The fuse here must be the fuse on an old-fashioned cannon. In Latin America, you might hear **a todo vapor** (*at full steam*).

**Subió las escaleras a toda mecha.**
She went up the stairs like greased lightning.

## irse pitando (Sp)

*"to go off whistling"*
= to take off like a shot
= to make tracks

This phrase refers to steam trains blowing their whistles as they leave the station. An equivalent expression, more widely used, is **irse volando** (*to go off flying*).

**Me voy pitando que se me hace tarde.**
I'm going to be late; I better make tracks.

# despedirse a la francesa (Sp)

*"to say goodbye in the French way"*
= to leave without saying goodbye

France once set the trend in etiquette for the rest of Europe. Supposedly, in the seventeenth century, it was de rigueur not to bid farewell when leaving upper-crust gatherings in Paris. Hence the expression.

**Una vez más se despidieron a la francesa.**
Yet again they left without saying goodbye.

# andando, que es gerundio (Sp)

*"going, which is gerund"*
= we'd better get moving

You use this phrase to hurry along somebody who is dawdling. The gerund in Spanish is the form of the verb ending in -*ndo*.

**¡Ya son las once! ¡Andando, que es gerundio!**
It's eleven already! We'd better get moving!

## salir como alma que lleva el diablo

> *"to leave like a soul that the Devil is carrying"*
> = to run away like a bat out of hell

● The Devil is always in a hurry, it seems, to rush your soul off to Hell.

**Cuando vio entrar a su ex, salió como alma que lleva el diablo.**
When he saw his ex come in, he ran away like a bat out of hell.

## ahuecar el ala

> *"to hollow the wing"*
> = to beat it

**Será mejor que ahuequemos el ala.**
We'd better beat it.

# hacer dedo

*"to do thumb"*

= to hitchhike

**Pensábamos hacer dedo hasta la playa.**
We were thinking of hitching to the beach.

## cortarse la coleta (Sp)

*"to cut off your pigtail"*
= to quit
= to retire

The pigtail is a bullfighting reference. At their last bullfight before retiring, bullfighters ceremonially cut off the false pigtail attached to their hat.

**Dijo que no pensaba cortarse la coleta todavía.**
He said he wasn't thinking of retiring yet.

# Chance, surprise, and the unexpected

## se le pusieron los ojos como platos

*"her/his eyes became like plates"*

= her/his eyes were nearly popping out of his/her head

A phrase that forcefully conveys the look on the face of somebody who is very surprised.

**Cuando vio el anillo, se le pusieron los ojos como platos.**
When she saw the ring, her eyes nearly popped out of her head.

## se me puso la piel de gallina

> *"I got chicken skin"*
> ≠ I got goose bumps

A similar image to English, but with a different bird.

**Se nos puso la piel de gallina cuando escuchamos el alarido.**
We got goose bumps when we heard the scream.


## por si las moscas

> *"just in case the flies"*
> = just in case
> = to be on the safe side

**Yo llamaría antes, por si las moscas.**
I'd call first, to be on the safe side.

## ¿qué aires te traen por aquí?

*"what breezes bring you here?"*
= what a surprise to see you here!
= what brings you here?

**¡Pero si es Alberto! ¿Qué aires te traen por aquí?**
Well, if it isn't Alberto! What brings you here?

## quedarse de piedra

*"to turn to stone"*
= to be stunned

Another expression with a similar meaning is **quedarse de helado** (*to freeze*).

**Cuando me contó que se había divorciado, me quedé de piedra.**
When he told me he'd gotten divorced, I was stunned.

# blanco como el papel

> *"white like paper"*
> = as white as a sheet

● To convey how the color drains from your face through shock and surprise, Spanish also refers to walls: **blanco como la pared** *(white like the wall)*.

**¿Qué te ha pasado? ¡Estás blanca como el papel!**
What's happened to you? You're as white as a sheet!

# como llovido del cielo

> *"as if rained from the sky"*
> = heaven-sent
> = a godsend

**Su ayuda nos vino como llovida del cielo.**
Her help was a godsend for us.

# quedarse bizco

*"to turn cross-eyed"*
= to be dumbstruck

● **Quedarse** is sometimes used to describe changes caused by external circumstances: **Se quedó viuda** (*She was widowed*).

**Me quedé bizco viéndola cocinar.**
I was dumbstruck when I watched her cook.

# Eating, drinking, drunkenness, and excess

## comer a dos carrillos (Sp)

"to eat with two cheeks"

= to stuff your face

**Estaban sentados a la mesa comiendo a dos carrillos.**
They were sitting at the table stuffing their faces.

## tener buen diente

*"to have a good tooth"*
= to be a hearty eater
= to have a healthy appetite

**He preparado bastante comida porque los invitados tienen buen diente.**
I've made quite a lot of food because the guests have healthy appetites.

## esto sabe a demonios *(Sp)*

*"this tastes of devils"*
= this tastes really awful

Few, if any, living people know what devils taste like, but it's a safe bet that they aren't exactly delicious.

**Este filete sabe a demonios.**
This steak tastes really awful.

## vivir a cuerpo de rey

*"to live like the body of a king"*
= to live like a king

● The Spanish phrase emphasizes the bodily indulgence and comforts of being a king.

**Vive a cuerpo de rey en casa de sus padres.**
He lives like a king at his parents' house.


## ponerse morado (Sp)

*"to go purple"*
= to stuff yourself

● An alternative to this expression is common in Latin America: empacharse (*to get indigestion*).

**Nos pusimos morados de comer cerezas.**
We stuffed ourselves with cherries.

## beber como una esponja

"*to drink like a sponge*"
= to drink like a fish

An alternative to this is **beber como un cosaco** (*to drink like a Cossack*).

**Tu tío bebe como una esponja.**
Your uncle drinks like a fish.

## borracho como una cuba

"*as drunk as a wine barrel*"
= totally plastered
= as drunk as a skunk

You can also simply say **como una cuba**.

**El conductor que provocó el accidente estaba borracho como una cuba.**
The driver who caused the accident was totally plastered.

## empinar el codo

"*to bend your elbow*"
= to hit the bottle

**Todos conocen su afición a empinar el codo.**
Everybody knows he likes hitting the bottle.

## en cantidades industriales

*"in industrial quantities"*
= by the basketful

**Había comida y bebida en cantidades industriales.**
There was food and drink by the basketful.

# Directness, decisiveness, and expressing opinions

## consultarlo con la almohada

*"to consult your pillow about it"*
= to sleep on it

**Voy a consultarlo con la almohada y mañana te doy una respuesta.**
I'm going to sleep on it, and I'll give you an answer tomorrow.

## echar sapos y culebras por la boca

*"to throw toads and snakes out of your mouth"*
= to swear up a storm
= to swear your head off
= to use very strong language

**Cuando entramos en la tienda, había un cliente echando sapos y culebras por la boca.**
When we went into the store, there was a customer swearing up a storm.

## al pan pan, y al vino vino

*"call bread bread and wine wine"*
= I believe in calling a spade a spade
= I'm not going to mince words

The Spanish staples of bread and wine provide the image for plain speaking.

**Al pan pan, y al vino vino: es un auténtico canalla.**
I'm not going to mince words: he's a real swine.

## no tener pelos en la lengua

> *"not to have hairs on your tongue"*
> = not to mince your words

If you had hairs on your tongue, it would be hard to say what you really mean.

**No tiene pelos en la lengua y siempre dice lo que piensa.**
He doesn't mince his words, and he always says what he thinks.

## hablar a calzón quitado

> *"to talk with your underpants off"*
> = to talk openly
> = to talk with no holds barred

**Los dos presidentes hablaron a calzón quitado sin la presencia de sus asistentes.**
The two presidents talked with no holds barred in the absence of their assistants.

## ¿a ti quién te dio vela en este entierro?

"who gave you a candle at this funeral?"

= what business is it of yours?

**¿A ti quién te dio vela en este entierro? Esta discusión no tiene nada que ver contigo.**
What business is it of yours? This argument has nothing to do with you.

## me salió del alma

"it came out from my soul"

= it just came out

= I said it without thinking

**Después me arrepentí, pero el insulto me salió del alma.**
I regretted it afterward, but the insult just came out.

## mentar la soga en casa del ahorcado

> *"to mention the rope in the house of the hanged man"*
> = to put your foot in your mouth

● This proverb was famously used by Don Quijote.

**Ni se te ocurra preguntar por su ex marido, no vayas a mentar la soga en casa del ahorcado.**
Don't even think about asking about her ex-husband. That would really be putting your foot in your mouth!

## nadar entre dos aguas

> *"to swim between two waters"*
> = to sit on the fence

**Siempre ha sido de los que nadan entre dos aguas sin comprometerse con nadie.**
He's always been one of those people who sit on the fence without committing to anybody.

## no saber a qué carta quedarse *(Sp)*

*"not to know which card to stay with"*

= not to know which to choose

An image from card games where you have to decide which cards to hang on to, and which to take from the pack.

**Las dos propuestas me parecen excelentes y no sé a qué carta quedarme.**

The two proposals look excellent to me, and I don't know which to choose.

## se cae por su propio peso

*"it falls from its own weight"*

= it goes without saying

The image in this pretty formal phrase suggests a ripe fruit ready to drop.

**Se cae por su propio peso que ahora deberíamos ayudarle nosotros.**

It goes without saying that we should help him now.

## ¡para el carro!

*"stop the cart!"*

= wait a minute!

= hold your horses!

**¡Para el carro! ¿De dónde va a salir el dinero para el viaje?**
Hold your horses! Where's the money for the trip going to come from?

# hablar del sexo de los ángeles (Sp)

*"to talk about the sex of the angels"*
= to continue pointless discussion

> This phrase clearly comes from the same medieval theological navel-gazing that gave English the similar phrase for pointless discussion: *How many angels can dance on the head of a pin?*

**Me parece que estamos hablando del sexo de los ángeles.**
I think it's pointless to continue this discussion.

# Money, debt, wealth, and poverty

# atan los perros con longaniza (Sp)

*"they tie up dogs with sausages"*
= the streets are paved with gold

● You'd have to be very rich to tie up dogs with sausages, as they'd only eat them. This phrase goes back to the eighteenth century, to a rich man's maid who really did tie up a dog with a string of sausages.

**Hay gente que se piensa que en este país atan los perros con longaniza.**
There are people who believe that the streets are paved with gold in this country.

## costar un ojo de la cara

> *"to cost an eye of your face"*
> = to cost an arm and a leg

● Another way to emphasize how much something cost you is to refer to another part of your body: **Me costó un riñón** (*It cost me a kidney*).

**El nuevo modelo cuesta un ojo de la cara.**
The new model costs an arm and a leg.

## criarse en buenos pañales (*Sp*)

> *"to be raised in good diapers"*
> = to be born with a silver spoon in your mouth

**Ese no sabe lo que es pasar hambre, se crió en buenos pañales.**
He doesn't know what it is to be hungry. He was born with a silver spoon in his mouth.

## el oro y el moro

> *"the gold and the Moor"*
> = too much

Long ago some Spaniards held two Moorish noblemen to ransom. The Spaniards were so greedy that even after getting the money they kept their captives, and thus became a byword for a large amount of money.

**Pedían el oro y el moro por una casita minúscula.**
They were asking too much for a tiny house.

## nadar en la abundancia

> *"to be swimming in abundance"*
> = to be rolling in cash

**En esta casa no se puede decir que nademos en la abundancia.**
It couldn't be said we're rolling in cash in this house.

## rascarse el bolsillo

> *"to scratch your pocket"*
> = to chip in
> = to make a contribution

**Pedro fue el único que no quiso rascarse el bolsillo.**
Pedro was the only one who refused to chip in.

## ponerse las botas (*Sp*)

> *"to put on boots"*
> = to be raking it in

Historically, only the rich could afford boots, hence the image of wealth this phrase suggests.

**Abrieron un bar en un lugar muy turístico y se pusieron las botas.**
They opened a bar in a tourist hot spot, and they raked it in.

# tirar la casa por la ventana

*"to throw the house through the window"*
= to spare no expense

This curious phrase originates from the Spanish lottery, first set up in the eighteenth century. Winners threw their old furniture out of the window to announce their new life was beginning. The custom survives on New Year's Eve in Naples, which was once under Spanish rule.

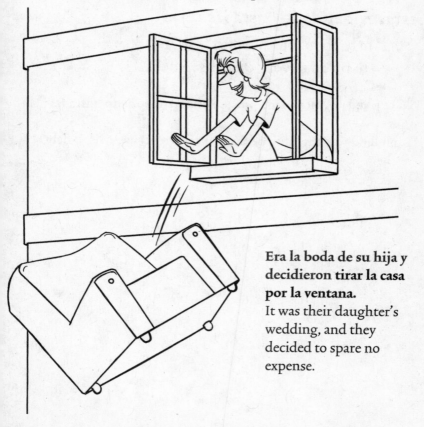

**Era la boda de su hija y decidieron tirar la casa por la ventana.**
It was their daughter's wedding, and they decided to spare no expense.

## parecer un muerto de hambre

> *"to look like a starved person"*
> = not to have a penny to your name

**Esos dos parecen muertos de hambre.**
Those two don't have a penny to their name.


## estar endeudado hasta las cejas

> *"to be up to your eyebrows in debt"*
> = to be up to your eyeballs in debt

**No te puedo prestar nada porque estoy endeudado hasta las cejas.**
I can't lend you anything because I'm up to my eyeballs in debt.

## no tener más que el día y la noche (Sp)

> *"to have only the day and the night"*
> = not to have two pennies to rub together

**No nos pidáis nada, no tenemos más que el día y la noche.**
Don't ask us for any anything; we don't have two pennies to rub together.

## no tener un cuarto

> *"not to have a 'cuarto'"*
> = to be broke

**Un cuarto** was a coin of low value used long ago in Spain. There are other variants of this expression, such as **no tener un céntimo** (*not to have a cent*). In Latin America, this expression varies from one country to another, depending on the currency.

**¿Me podrías invitar? No tengo un cuarto.**
Could you treat me? I'm broke.

# Language, speech, silence, and conversation

## coserse la boca

*"to sew up your mouth"*
= to keep your lips sealed

**Y será mejor que te cosas la boca.**
You'd better keep your lips sealed.

## hablar por los codos

> *"to talk through your elbows"*
> = to talk a mile a minute

**Ten cuidado con él porque habla por los codos.**
Careful with him because he talks a mile a minute.

## enrollarse como una persiana

> *"to roll up like a blind"*
> = to go on and on

**Me da miedo hablar con él porque siempre se enrolla como una persiana.**
I'm wary of talking to him because he always goes on and on.

# hablar en cristiano

*"to speak in Christian"*
= to speak in plain Spanish

At one time, much of Spain was ruled by Moorish Arabs, and there was also a large Jewish community. Christian Spanish-speakers equated their own language with Christianity, as opposed to what the Arabs or Sephardic Jews spoke.

**A mí háblame en cristiano, que no entiendo nada de lo que dices.**
Talk to me in plain English; I can't understand a word of what you're saying.

# no decir chus ni mus (*Sp*)

*"to say neither chus nor mus"*
= not to say a word

**Chus** doesn't mean anything on its own outside this phrase. There is a card game called **mus**, but the use of the word here is probably to create a rhyme. You often hear a less colorful version of this expression: **no decir ni mu**.

**Intenté sonsacarle lo que sabía pero no dijo ni chus ni mus.**
I tried to worm out of him what he knew, but he didn't say a word.

## no despegar los labios

*"not to unstick your lips"*

= not to utter a single word

**No despegó los labios** durante toda la reunión.
He didn't utter a single word the whole meeting.

## seré una tumba

*"I'll be a tomb"*

= I won't breathe a word

**No te preocupes, seré una tumba.**
Don't worry, I won't breathe a word.

# meter la cuchara

*"to put in your spoon"*
= to butt in
= to stick your nose in other people's business

● People used to eat from a communal stewpot by dipping their spoons into it. From that comes the idea of sticking your nose into a conversation.

**Siempre tienes que meter la cuchara.**
You always have to butt in.

# no decir esta boca es mía

*"not to say this mouth is mine"*

= not to say a word

**Si me preguntan, no pienso decir esta boca es mía.**
If they ask me, I don't intend to say a word.

# Youth, experience, age, and death

## estar todavía en pañales

*"to be still in diapers"*

= to be wet behind the ears

**Es inteligente, pero todavía está en pañales.**
She's bright, but she's still a bit wet
behind the ears.

## estar en la edad del pavo (Sp)

"*to be at the age of the turkey*"
= to be at that awkward age

The Latin American expression is closer to the English: **estar en la edad de la bobera** (*to be at the age of silliness*).

**No le hagas mucho caso porque está en la edad del pavo.**
Don't take any notice of her; she's at that awkward age.

## peinar canas

"*to comb gray hair*"
= to be getting on in years

Spanish expresses the concept of *gray hair* with the plural word **las canas**.

**Lo intenta ocultar pero ya peina canas.**
He tries to hide it, but he's getting on in years.

## criar gusanos (Sp)

*"to grow worms"*
= to be pushing up daisies

**El dictador cría gusanos en este cementerio.**
The dictator is pushing up daisies in this cemetery.

## estirar la pata

*"to stretch your leg"*
= to kick the bucket

**Hace ahora un año que estiró la pata.**
It's a year now since he kicked the bucket.

## a la vejez viruelas

*"to old age, smallpox"*
= imagine that happening at his/her age

You use this phrase to show your surprise when somebody of a certain age does something unexpected.

**Todos los fines de semana se va a subir montañas.**
**–¡A la vejez, viruelas!**
Every weekend he heads off to go and climb mountains. – Imagine that, at his age!

## ha llovido mucho desde entonces

*"it's rained a lot since then"*
= a lot of water has flowed under the bridge since
then

**En aquella época éramos muy amigos, pero ha llovido mucho desde entonces.**
We were great friends in those days, but a lot of water has flowed under the bridge since then.

# Index

## Uu

## Vv

## Zz